Novels for Students, Volume 27

Project Editor: Ira Mark Milne Rights Acquisition and Management: Vernon English, Leitha Etheridge-Sims, Aja Perales, Sue Rudolph Composition: Evi Abou-El-Seoud Manufacturing: Drew Kalasky

Imaging: Lezlie Light

Product Design: Pamela A. E. Galbreath, Jennifer Wahi Content Conversion: Civie Green, Katrina Coach Product Manager: Meggin Condino © 2008 Gale, Cengage Learning

For product information and technology assistance, contact us at
Gale Customer Support, 1-800-877-4253.
For permission to use material from this text or product,
submit all requests online at
www.cengage.com/permissions.
Further permissions questions can be emailed to
permissionrequest@cengage.com While every effort has been made to ensure the reliability of the information presented in this publication, Gale, a part of Cengage Learning, does not guarantee the accuracy of the data contained herein. Gale accepts no payment for listing; and inclusion in the publication of any organization, agency, institution, publication, service, or individual does not imply endorsement of the editors or publisher. Errors brought to the attention of the publisher and verified to the satisfaction of the publisher will be corrected in future editions.

Gale
27500 Drake Rd.
Farmington Hills, MI, 48331-3535

ISBN-13: 978-0-7876-8684-0
ISBN-10: 0-7876-8684-0

ISSN 1094-3552

This title is also available as an e-book.
ISBN-13: 978-1-4144-3831-3
ISBN-10: 1-4144-3831-1
Contact your Gale, a part of Cengage Learning sales
representative for ordering information.

Printed in the United States of America
1 2 3 4 5 6 7 12 11 10 09 08

Life of Pi

Yann Martel 2001

Introduction

Considered most simply, Yann Martel's acclaimed novel, *Life of Pi* (2001), can be described as a postcolonial novel, focusing on the culture and stories of a former British colony (in this case, India.) But to see this novel only as a postcolonial story is to limit its possibilities. Set against the backdrop of a period of Indian history known as the Emergency, the novel opens in the southern Indian city of Pondicherry, which was once the capital of French India, and the story explores the tensions facing this tiny city during a time of deep political turmoil. In the midst of this, the protagonist, Piscine Patel (known as Pi) emigrates from India to Canada with his family. They leave India by boat, but the ship sinks on the way. Pi and a Bengal tiger are the only survivors. As Pi struggles to coexist on a lifeboat with a tiger, he comes to understand the human condition. Indeed, Martel's novel quickly changes from a postcolonial novel to a deep meditation on the complex nature of faith, morality, and, ultimately, identity. The story also stands as an argument for the existence of God, or at least for sustaining belief in that existence.

A recent edition of the novel was published by Vintage Canada in 2002.

Author Biography

Yann Martel was born in Salamanca, Spain, on June 25, 1963, to Canadian parents. Soon after the birth of their son, Martel's parents joined the

Canadian Foreign Service, and the family traveled often, living in Alaska, Costa Rica, France, Mexico, and a number of Canadian provinces. Martel continued to travel well into his adulthood, spending time in Iran, Turkey, and India before returning to Canada to study philosophy at Trent University in Ontario. After graduating from Trent in 1986, he worked variously as a tree planter, dishwasher, and security guard while developing his writing.

With years of travel and writing behind him, Martel published his first book in 1993, a collection of short fiction titled *The Facts Behind the Helsinki Roccamatios*. The stories focus on such themes as illness, the anguish of youth, grief, and death. The collection was awarded the 1993 Journey Prize in Canada, and was followed in 1996 by his first novel, *Self*, a story of shifting identities. Martel's first novel was on the short list for the Chapters/Books in Canada First Novel Award.

In 2002, Martel was recognized internationally when his second novel, *Life of Pi* (2001), was awarded the Man Booker Prize for Fiction, the Boeke Prize (South Africa), and the Hugh MacLennan Prize for Fiction (Canada). The novel was also short listed for the prestigious Governor General's Literary Award for Fiction (Canada) and The Commonwealth Writers Prize (Eurasia Region, Best Book). The accolades continued into 2003, with *Life of Pi* being selected as the recipient of the Quality Paperback Book Club's annual New Voices Award. The novel has been translated into more than thirty languages, has found readers in more than forty countries, and has been optioned for film adaptation. Notably, the French-Canadian edition of the novel was translated by Martel's own parents, Nicole and Emile.

Martel followed this remarkable success with a collection of short stories, *We Ate the Children Last*, in 2004. In April, 2007, Martel returned to prominence when he began a very public and much publicized project to mail the Prime Minister of Canada, Stephen Harper, a new book every two weeks. Martel noted that he hoped to help the political leader expand upon a sense of what the author called "stillness." The three initial mailings, for instance, were Leo Tolstoy's *The Death of Ivan Ilych*, George Orwell's *Animal Farm*, and Agatha Christie's *The Murder of Roger Ackroyd*. Martel spends his time between creative projects in Montreal, Quebec, and he also serves as writer-in-residence with the English department at the University of Saskatchewan.

Author's Note

A brief, italicized section establishes some background on the author of the novel, who is also a character in the text of the novel itself. (Each of the author's sections are similarly italicized, setting them off visually as well as thematically from the rest of the novel.) Confiding that he flew to Bombay in order to rejuvenate his mind and his writing following the lukewarm response to his first two books, the author is forced to admit, too, that he is suffering from writer's block. Leaving Bombay for a period of intellectual and spiritual wandering, he ends up in the small southern Indian city of Pondicherry, which had for many years been the centerpiece of "that most modest of colonial empires, *French* India."

Visiting a local coffee shop, the author has a chance encounter with a small elderly man, Francis Adirubasamy, who promises to tell him "a story that will make you believe in God." Taking notes of the fragmented tale that unfolds during their conversation, the author finds the story magnetic and it continues to fascinate him after he returns to Toronto. Searching for the protagonist of Adirubasamy's story, the author tracks down and speaks at length with Mr. Piscine Patel, whose story is told in the bulk of the novel. The author's conclusion, and his aim in writing the novel, is made very clear: "It seemed natural," he concludes, "that Mr. Patel's story should be told mostly in the first person, in his voice and through his eyes." At the same time, the author is quick to point out, "any inaccuracies or mistakes" that might find their way into the story are the responsibility of the author.

Part One: Toronto and Pondicherry

Chapter 1

The main narrative begins with Piscine (Pi) Patel's declaration that his early life had been one of great suffering, the cause of which is never made clear. Nonetheless, this suffering leaves the youthful Pi oscillating in emotion between sadness and despondency. His mood lifts, and his life takes a turn for the better, when he decides to commit his energies to the study of two different topics: religious studies and zoology. Speaking at length about his research into sloths, Pi uses the discussion to hint at a number of facts that will appear in subsequent chapters: that he misses India; that he misses someone named Richard Parker; and that he has spent an extended period of time in a Mexican hospital suffering variously from anemia and dehydration.

Chapter 2

In a very brief chapter, the author reenters the narrative with details about where Pi currently lives in Toronto, what he looks like, and the way he speaks.

Chapter 3

The chapter discusses the history of Pi's full name, Piscine, which came from the name of the pool where a family friend, Francis Adirubasamy (whom Pi calls Mamaji), taught Pi to swim. Pi is the only member in his family who is not afraid of the water, and he has an almost obsessive love for the ritualistic nature of swimming. Readers learn details, too, about Adirubasamy's own life as a champion swimmer and later as a student in Paris.

Media Adaptations

- HarperCollins released an audio version of the novel (read by Kerry Shale) in 2003.

Chapter 4

Pi shares a series of reflections upon his childhood in India. Most tellingly, he speaks about growing up as the son of a zookeeper, Santosh Patel. Pi's father ran the famous zoo at Pondicherry. As a child, Pi considered the zoo to be a kind of paradise in which various rituals and an almost clock-like precision combine to create a logical world of balance and coexistence. Pi also offers a lengthy and detailed defense of the practice and philosophy of zoo keeping, which is grounded in a complex balancing of respectful stewardship, authoritative control of territory, and applied theory. Sadly, Pi concludes, zoos have fallen into disrepute in the contemporary world.

Chapter 5

Teased at school because of his name (Piscine became Pissing), Pi gets the teachers and his fellow students to call him by the shortened (and geometrically significant) name of Pi. In his renaming, Pi finds a new beginning: "And so, in that Greek letter that looks like a shack with a corrugated tin roof, in that elusive, irrational number with which scientists try to understand the universe, I found refuge," he declares.

Chapter 6

In another brief chapter, the author interjects once again to talk about Pi's love of food, his excellent cooking, and his exotic and well-stocked kitchen.

Chapter 7

Returning to Pi's recollections of life in Pondicherry, this chapter opens a series of chapters that catalogue a number of important people, moments, and ideas that shape Pi as he matures. This chapter focuses on the influence of Mr. Satish Kumar, Pi's biology teacher, an avowed atheist, and an active Communist. He visits the zoo often, seeing it as a reassuring embodiment of the powers of reason and logic over the chaos of the natural world.

Chapter 8

After commenting at length on the cruelty that defines the relationships between animals in the natural order of things, Pi notes that the most dangerous animal is the human animal. In one of the more shocking scenes of the novel, Pi is also taught a powerful lesson when his father feeds a live goat to a caged tiger in order to demonstrate the dangers posed by wild animals, and the need for man to position himself as the dominant animal in any inter-species relationship. The keys to securing this balance of power are laid out clearly for Pi: understand how each animal responds to a potential threat or enemy; create a safe distance between yourself and that animal; be sure that each animal has sufficient food and water; and, most importantly, watch and learn the tendencies of each animal.

Chapter 9

Following a chapter on the dangers inherent in the relationship between humans and animals, Pi reflects on what he considers to be the strategy at the heart of zookeeping: nurturing animals so they get used to the presence of humans.

Chapter 10

In this brief chapter, Pi explains that even in the best of zoos there are animals that will try to escape. His point is clear: "animals don't escape *to somewhere* but *from something*."

Chapter 11

Continuing from chapter 10, Pi discusses a number of anecdotes about escaped zoo animals.

Chapter 12

Continuing his reflections from chapter 2, the author again speaks of Pi's cooking, with particular attention to the effects that the Indian man's spices have had on his untrained digestive tract. As an aside, the author notes that the mysterious Richard Parker is still often on Pi's mind, even so many years after their adventure together.

Chapter 13

Refocusing to the dynamics of animals and their territory, Pi talks about the example of a circus trainer and how he establishes the circus ring as his territory. By doing so, Pi argues, the trainer establishes himself at the top of the animal hierarchy.

Chapter 14

This chapter continues the discussion of circus trainers and their control of the animals in their ring.

Chapter 15

The author steps forward once again to describe Pi's house in Toronto, which is described in detail as containing a blend of religious icons and art from Hindu, Islamic, and Christian traditions.

Chapter 16

Pi explains his youthful relationship with the three major religions that shaped his ideas about the world. Born into a Hindu family, he describes his almost insatiable hunger for Prasad (an offering to God) and the ways that his hands almost automatically would fall into the prayer position. More importantly, he points out, is the Hindu philosophy of life, which he will always hold, he claims, as the centerpiece of his religious beliefs: "That which sustains the universe beyond thought and language, and that which is at the core of us and struggles for expression, is the same thing."

Chapter 17

Pi then goes on to recount the story of his almost casual introduction to Christianity. Stepping into a local church one day, the fourteen-year-old Pi enters into a discussion with Father Martin, who tells the young Hindu the story of the crucifixion of Christ. When pushed to explicate the deepest meaning of the story, Father Martin explains to Pi that the main idea shaping the stories of Christianity is always the same: love. Following some days of reflection, Pi decides that he will become a Christian. To Pi, this does not mean that he will no longer be a Hindu. In fact, he intends to be both.

Chapter 18

As Pi states almost casually, "Islam followed right behind" his decision to accept Christianity. Pi meets a Muslim mystic and baker who also becomes the second person named Satish Kumar to enter Pi's life.

Chapter 19

Through the second Mr. Kumar, the young Hindu/Christian comes to be intrigued by the daily rituals of Islam and by the stories of Mohammed that the baker shares with him.

Chapter 20

In this chapter, Pi comes to understand religious belief as a series of stories developed by humans in order to make their lives more understandable, more readily explainable, and generally more meaningful.

Chapter 21

This chapter opens with the author sitting in a café, reflecting on the story he is being told and, less comfortably, the "glum contentment" that has come to characterize his own life. Significantly, he remembers two phrases that had particularly intrigued him from his most recent conversation with Pi: "dry, yeastless factuality" and "the better story." Both of these phrases echo again and again as the novel unfolds.

Chapter 22

Referring to the previous phrases, Pi imagines the final words of an atheist versus those of an agnostic. Pi indicates that while an atheist would likely undergo a last-minute conversion as he experiences death, the agnostic would likely try to explain the experience in scientific terms.

Chapter 23

Pi recounts an episode where a representative from each of Pi's religions approach his parents. They state that a combination of faiths is not possible and that Pi must choose a single religion and a single mode of worship. His parents are shocked, for this is the first time they have even heard of their son's fascination with religion. Arguing that people who use the name of God to support violence or factionalism do not understand the word of God, Pi answers his challengers with a simple yet profound idea: he just wants to love God.

Chapter 24

In this brief chapter, Pi's brother, Ravi, teases Pi mercilessly upon discovering Pi's religious views.

Chapter 25

In this chapter, Pi recounts how people from the various religious groups react negatively to his complex spiritual quest.

Chapter 26

Now that his parents know about his religious beliefs, Pi asks them to allow him to be baptized and to have a prayer rug of his own. After some attempts to dissuade their son, his parents give in to both requests, marking the end of this early stage of Pi's spiritual journey.

Chapter 27

Pi's parents discuss, with some humor, the spiritual route chosen by their youngest son.

Chapter 28

Upon getting a prayer rug and a baptism, Pi feels that both events combine to give him a rejuvenating cleansing that he compares to a monsoon rain.

Chapter 29

The focal point of the novel shifts dramatically from religion to politics when Pi's father announces that the political situation in India during the time of the Emergency has effectively ruined the business of the Pondicherry zoo. Thus, Pi's father has decided that the zoo animals will be sold and that the family will emigrate to Canada.

Chapter 30

The author begins this chapter with a declarative statement: "He's married." Upon being introduced to Pi's wife, Meena, the author begins to see the house in a new light, paying attention to items and details that had gone unnoticed during his previous visits. His view has been limited, the author is forced to acknowledge, because he was not looking closely enough for details that might illuminate more clearly the corners and edges of the story he is being told.

It seems that even the author must admit to himself that a story (in this case, the story about Pi) can change drastically depending on the details that one chooses to pay attention to. This is an important revelation in that it anticipates the final section, when two versions of the same story are presented. Each story shares the same basic details (a boat sank, there are a certain number of survivors, the survivors die off in a certain order, etc.). However, each story presents those details through a distinct and often contradictory lens.

Chapter 31

Pi recounts the one-time meeting of the two Misters Kumar (one an atheist, the other a Muslim mystic). Joining Pi for a tour of the zoo, the two men see a zebra for the first time. Both are in awe of the exotic creature, and try to explain its marvelous markings.

Chapter 32

Pi takes this discussion as an opportunity to discuss zoomorphism, which is what happens when an animal takes a human being or any other animal outside of its species to be one of its own. Pi also speculates as to the psychological and emotional causes of this phenomenon.

Chapter 33

The author recalls the time he has spent with Pi exploring Pi's very minimal family memorabilia, including photos of weddings, the Pondicherry zoo, and the (still) mysterious Richard Parker. The chapter closes with Pi lamenting that he has lost so many of his memories, most sadly those of his mother, Gita, of whom he does not even have a picture. "It's very sad not to remember what your mother looks like," Pi says sadly, closing the book that contains images of his past.

Chapter 34

In preparation for the move across the Pacific, Pi's father sells off many of the zoo animals, agreeing to oversee the transport of the remainder in the same cargo ship that will carry his family to their new life in Canada. Pi reflects upon the fact that some animals are in high demand, while others are more or less ignored. He compares the inspections of the animals prior to receiving transport papers to the preparations of his own family to leave Pondicherry.

Chapter 35

Pi describes the mixed emotions with which the family leaves India aboard the Japanese ship *Tsimtsum* on June 21, 1977. He talks about packing the animals into cargo as well as his philosophy of how a person deals with life when things do not turn out as planned.

Chapter 36

The first part of the book ends as the author remembers his first meeting with Pi's two children, Usha and Nikhil. Now that the author has met Pi's family, but with much of Pi's story yet to be told, the author closes the chapter by stating: "This story has a happy ending."

Part Two: The Pacific Ocean

Chapter 37

Part Two opens with the sinking of the *Tsimtsum*, which leaves Pi suddenly separated from his family, floating in a lifeboat with an injured zebra. He sees Richard Parker, a 450-pound Bengal tiger, swimming toward the lifeboat. Rather than share the boat with a huge Bengal tiger, Pi leaps overboard.

Chapter 38

In a flashback to the moments preceding the sinking of the ship, Pi remembers his excitement at the possibilities that await him and his brother in Canada. His optimism turns to confusion when he feels the ship shudder with an explosion, and then to fear as he witnesses the chaos unfolding around him.

Chapter 39

Tossed into a lifeboat, Pi finds himself joined

suddenly by an injured zebra.

Chapter 40

Picking up where he left off in chapter 37, Pi recognizes his dilemma: stay in the water with the sharks that are beginning to gather, or climb back aboard the lifeboat, where Richard Parker has taken refuge under a tarpaulin.

Chapter 41

Having climbed back aboard the lifeboat, Pi watches as the ship sinks. He also realizes that he is sharing his new home with not only a tiger and an injured zebra, but also with a mean-spirited hyena.

Chapter 42

A Borneo orangutan named Orange Juice floats by the boat on a raft of bananas. Pi rescues Orange Juice from the disintegrating raft of fruit, but forgets to bring any of the bananas aboard.

Chapter 43

Pi begins to establish the power structure within the group of animals aboard the lifeboat. His most immediate threat is the hyena, which is racing in circles around the boat.

Chapter 44

During his first night aboard the lifeboat, the hyena kills the injured zebra, as a terrified Pi listens helplessly from his end of the boat.

Chapter 45

The following morning, Pi contemplates the meaning of life and death as it is now presented to him. He also watches Orange Juice's reaction to recent events.

Chapter 46

What Pi sees at first fascinates him, as Orange Juice raises herself to her full height to intimidate the hyena into submission. Violence is averted this time, but Pi is aware that the peace aboard the lifeboat is temporary.

Chapter 47

As sharks circle the lifeboat, Pi watches once again as violence breaks out, this time between the still ravenous hyena and Orange Juice. He is surprised and somewhat appalled as the orangutan attempts to club the hyena to death. In the end, Orange Juice dies, and Pi is left in an almost delirious state of fear that he will be the next victim.

Chapter 48

Pi recalls the clerical error that led to the tiger being named Richard Parker instead of Thirsty, which was the animal's intended name.

Chapter 49

The story resumes with Pi tentatively exploring the boat in search of water and supplies. He must remain aware at all times, he knows, of the location of both the murderous hyena and the quiet, but always dangerous, Richard Parker.

Chapter 50

This relatively brief chapter is dedicated to a detailed description of the physical dimensions of the lifeboat and the equipment discovered in it.

Chapter 51

Discovering the rations in the boat, Pi finds his spirits uplifted. He calculates that he has enough food and water to last for 124 days.

Chapter 52

This chapter is dedicated almost totally to recounting the list of items that Pi discovers aboard the lifeboat.

Chapter 53

Awakening to what he calls "the reality of Richard Parker," Pi prepares himself to battle the animals that share his limited space. When Richard Parker raises his powerful body to attack, Pi is certain that he is the intended victim. He is surprised, relieved, and somewhat horrified when the tiger instead kills the hyena.

Certain that he will be next to die, Pi is saved when a rat scrambles over the tarpaulin and climbs onto Pi's head. Grabbing the rat, Pi throws it to the tiger, who accepts the offering. Pi senses that a balance has been reached between them, for the moment at least.

Chapter 54

Pi contemplates the pros and cons of each of

six plans for dealing with Richard Parker, ranging from pushing him off the lifeboat to waging a war of attrition that will end with one of them dying from starvation or dehydration.

Chapter 55

Thinking and thinking again about each of his six plans, Pi settles momentarily on the plan to outwait Richard Parker and hope that he starves to death. Pi immediately recognizes the faulty logic and inevitable failure of this plan.

Chapter 56

In this brief but important chapter, Pi reflects upon the nature of fear, which he classifies as "life's only true opponent."

Chapter 57

Ironically, the presence of Richard Parker calms Pi during their initial days aboard the lifeboat. Watching the tiger rest under his tarpaulin, Pi thinks back on what he has learned about circus trainers and decides to train the tiger rather than compete with him.

Chapter 58

Pi details the wealth of practical information that he discovers in a survival manual he finds in the lifeboat.

Chapter 59

Learning a variety of strategies for marking his territory aboard the lifeboat, Pi begins training

Richard Parker. More importantly, he discovers and learns to operate a solar still that can convert salt water into the drinkable water that he will need to survive. He also knows that the ocean around him is literally teeming with fish and turtles, both of which might prove a regular form of sustenance if he can figure out a method of catching them.

Chapter 60

Pi reflects upon the various life lessons learned during his spiritual development.

Chapter 61

Learning to catch fish, Pi also learns that food can be used as a training tool when dealing with Richard Parker. Pi further learns that he can adjust quite readily to killing another living creature in order to keep himself alive (Pi was previously a vegetarian). Upon this discovery Pi begins to deeply question his faith. The longer Pi is left to float upon the Pacific, the more his questioning will continue to deepen.

Chapter 62

The routine of catching food and making fresh water in the solar still occupies Pi's days at sea.

Chapter 63

Comparing himself to other famous survivors of lengthy sea journeys, Pi recounts an average day on the lifeboat. He juxtaposes this new routine with the increasingly fragile condition of his memories of life in India.

Chapter 64

This brief chapter details the physical ailments that begin to affect Pi as the days wear on.

Chapter 65

Believing firmly that knowledge will be crucial to his survival, Pi spends hours trying to decipher the navigational instructions in the survival manual. In the end, he is not successful.

Chapter 66

In this chapter, Pi recounts in detail how he came to master the techniques of hunting and killing fish and turtles. They are the basis of his entire diet, and Richard Parker's, as Pi shares all of his food with the tiger.

Chapter 67

Pi watches the small sea creatures that attach themselves to the lifeboat, recognizing that as he struggles to survive in inhospitable circumstances, he does so just above a complete, self-supporting ecosystem.

Chapter 68

Pi describes his sleeping patterns and Richard Parker's sleeping patterns.

Chapter 69

Pi spends his nights watching for a distant light, shooting flares in the hopes of attracting the attention of what he imagines to be ships passing nearby. As both he and Richard Parker watch the flares sink into the horizon, Pi realizes the futility of his efforts and the overwhelming barrenness of the ocean that surrounds him.

Chapter 70

Pi relates details of butchering a turtle. The chapter closes with Pi's determination to carve out his territory from Richard Parker once and for all.

Chapter 71

Pi makes a list of essentials for survival, which he offers as advice for anyone who might find themselves in a similar situation. The list has nine points.

Chapter 72

Richard Parker's training begins with Pi experimenting with various styles of shields, a piece of equipment that he feels will be necessary for the exercise he is about to undertake.

Chapter 73

Pi wishes for a book other than the survival manual. He also begins keeping a diary, written in tiny letters and detailing his feelings as well as the practical considerations of each day.

Chapter 74

Pi recounts how he maintains his religious rituals during the early days of his journey.

Chapter 75

In this one-sentence long chapter, Pi believes it is around the time of his mother's birthday, so he sings to celebrate it.

Chapter 76

Pi recalls how he got in the habit of cleaning up the feces left by the tiger, and how his own constipation was a source of great pain.

Chapter 77

As the rations aboard the lifeboat dwindle, Pi begins to deteriorate physically and mentally. He finds himself increasingly obsessed with food and water.

Chapter 78

Pi reflects upon the nature of the sky when seen from the point of view of a castaway. He also reflects on the loneliness of his position.

Chapter 79

This chapter is dedicated to sharks: how to capture them, how to butcher them, how they fight each other, and Pi's general observations of the various species.

Chapter 80

Opening with a discussion of the dorado (the most common fish that Pi catches), this chapter shifts gradually towards a meditation on Pi's interactions with Richard Parker and on the strength of the human mind to endure the most grueling of challenges.

Chapter 81

Pi acknowledges that the story of his survival might appear unbelievable to many people. He counters this disbelief by detailing a number of the key reasons why people should believe him.

Chapter 82

Pi again recounts the routine of gathering rainwater and food. He also shares more on the patterns that sustain both man and tiger in a variety of ways.

Chapter 83

A tremendous storm hits, and the lifeboat is tossed from wave to wave. Both Pi and Richard Parker struggle to remain upright in the boat, which begins to disintegrate in the ferocity of the storm. Terrified, the two passengers survive the storm.

Chapter 84

Following the storm, Pi again takes to recounting the setting in which he finds himself. Here marks on whales and dolphins, as well as how he ingeniously captures and kills a large sea bird for food.

Chapter 85

This brief chapter is dedicated to exploring the different responses of man and tiger to the occasional lightning storms that sweep over the small boat.

Chapter 86

In a brief but futile moment of hope, Pi spots a ship moving towards them. Planning the details of their rescue, Pi is aware suddenly that the huge ship is bearing down on them with no sign of slowing down or stopping. Almost overturned when the ship passes them by, the lifeboat continues to drift. Pi and Richard Parker both seem to give up hope.

Chapter 87

Pi recalls one of his favorite means of mental escape during his time on the lifeboat—choking himself almost to the point of unconsciousness.

Chapter 88

The lifeboat drifts through some trash. Pi snags a bottle, into which he places a note before launching it back into the sea.

Chapter 89

Pi reaches the lowest point of his journey. Without sufficient food or water, he begins to sleep more and more. When he does awaken, he has no energy, and he gives himself over to thoughts of death. He quits writing in his diary.

Chapter 90

Physically broken down to the point of blindness, Pi declines into a state of delirium. Hearing a voice with a French accent that he believes at first to be that of Parker, Pi encounters, or so he believes, another castaway adrift at sea. Indeed, it is not clear if the incident is real or imagined. The castaway is alone, and he is blind like Pi. The two men talk about food, which gradually leads the Frenchman to confess that he killed and cannibalized his shipmates (a man and a woman). When the Frenchman boards Pi's lifeboat with the intention of making Pi his next victim, he is immediately killed and eaten by the starving tiger.

Chapter 91

After rinsing his eyes with seawater, Pi regains his vision, sees the butchered body and, in a moment of extreme desperation, dries small strips of its flesh for his own consumption.

Chapter 92

Making "an exceptional botanical discovery," Pi and Parker come across a low-lying island made of algae that is drifting freely upon the sea. Beaching the lifeboat, Pi finds that the island has plentiful fresh water, fruit, and fish. It is also populated, he discovers, by a massive colony of meerkats who, Pi realizes, have come to understand the intricacies of the strange island's ecosystem.

And it is this ecosystem that is problematic, as Pi soon discovers. Upon realizing that the algae comprising the island floor turns toxic at night, Pi takes to sleeping in the trees with the meerkats. One day, discovering a tree that bears fruit-like objects containing human teeth, Pi concludes that his island paradise is carnivorous, and that eventually he, too, will be absorbed by the toxic algae as food for the island itself.

Chapter 93

Stocking the lifeboat with water and food, Pi and Parker set off once again in the lifeboat. Seeing all of his efforts as pointless and futile, Pi gives himself over to God's will by way of easing his suffering and desperation.

Chapter 94

Drifting for days, the two are finally washed ashore in Mexico. As Pi clambers onto the beach and collapses onto the sand, Parker disappears into the jungle. Pi is haunted by the suddenness of Parker's departure, and the fact that the two voyagers never had a proper farewell.

Discovered by local villagers, Pi is taken to an infirmary where he is nursed back to health.

Part Three: Benito Juárez Infirmary, Tomatlán, Mexico

Chapter 95

After returning to the voice of the author, he recounts the appearance of two officials from the Maritime Department in the Japanese Ministry of Transport, Tomohiro Okamoto and Atsuro Chiba. Traveling in California on unrelated business, they are redirected to Mexico to interview the sole survivor of the sinking of the *Tsimtsum*. After a confused journey to the small village, the men begin to interview Pi as he recuperates. Much of the conversation is presented in the form of interview transcripts.

Chapter 96

Introducing themselves to Pi, the two investigators give him a cookie and invite him to recount the details of the ship's explosion and his journey. Pi is happy to oblige their request.

Chapter 97

This two-word chapter simply says "The story," as Pi presumably recounts what the reader has already been told.

Chapter 98

The investigators take a break to consider the implications of the story.

Chapter 99

Pi is told by the Japanese investigators that his story is entertaining but wholly unbelievable. They push him to tell them what really happened during his 227 days at sea. At first, Pi challenges the men for their doubts, but gradually comes to recognize what they really desire to hear: "I know what you want," he says one day. "You want a story that won't surprise you. That will confirm what you already know. That won't make you see higher or further or differently. You want a flat story," he challenges them. "An immobile story. You want dry, yeastless factuality."

With this understanding, Pi tells the Japanese men another story. In this version, there are three other occupants in the lifeboat with Pi: his mother, a foul-mannered French cook, and a beautiful, young

Chinese sailor. When the sailor dies from injuries that are exacerbated by the cook's attacks upon him, he is used for food by the Frenchman, much to the disgust of Pi and his mother, who attempt to intervene. The Frenchman then kills Pi's mother before being killed by Pi himself. Pi survives his journey, he tells the investigators, by eating the flesh and organs of the murdered Frenchman. If one considers the order and manner in which these deaths occur, they largely mirror the deaths of the animals as Pi had earlier described. Looked at this way, the Frenchman is the hyena who kills the sailor (the zebra), and then Pi's mother (the orangutan), before being killed by Pi (the tiger).

Appalled at the savagery of the second story, but also aware of the parallels connecting the two versions of the tale, Okamoto and Chiba continue to question Pi and to debate over which story they will file in their official report.

Chapter 100

The senior investigator, Okamoto, is charged with filing the report, which comprises the final chapter of the novel. Okamoto settles on the story that includes Richard Parker. He does so because Pi asks the investigators which story is "better," and they respond that the "better story" is the one with the animals. Pi replies: "And so it goes with God." Here, Pi slyly indicates that the story of a world where God exists is better than the story of a world where God does not exist. Like Pi's stories of survival, one version is less believable than the other, but the less believable version is more thrilling than its counterpart. Thus, as Francis Adirubasamy promises the author at the beginning of the book, Pi's story is "a story that will make you believe in God."

Okamota therefore chooses the version of Pi's story that reaffirms belief in the existence of God. He notes, too, that Pi's tale "is an astounding story of courage and endurance" and that it "is unparalleled in the history of shipwrecks."

Francis Adirubasamy

Sitting in a Pondicherry coffee shop, Francis Adirubasamy is the elderly man who promises to tell the author a story that "will make [him] believe in God." He is, in other words, the catalyst for the novel that is about to unfold. At the same time, he is a character involved in Pi's childhood, the man who teaches Pi to swim and who is influential in naming the young protagonist. There is a closeness and a respect connecting Pi with Francis Adirubasamy; throughout the novel Pi refers to him as "Mamaji," which means "respected uncle."

The Author

The voice of the author surfaces at various points throughout the novel, commenting on Pi as he lives in the present-day city of Toronto while serving as the conduit for the story of Pi's journey with Richard Parker. A frustrated writer, the author is himself a student of storytelling who reflects on the tales laid out before him by Pi Patel.

The Blind Frenchman

The blind Frenchman is the castaway that Pi Patel meets in the midst of his most intense delusions at sea. Whether the blind Frenchman actually exists or is a figment of Pi's imagination is not clear. The blind Frenchman is, like Pi, delirious and hungry. He is also a storyteller, who recounts his own tale of murder and cannibalism. After boarding Pi's lifeboat with the intention of killing and eating Pi, he is instead eaten by the now ravenous Richard Parker.

Atsuro Chiba

One of the Japanese investigators from the Maritime Department in the Japanese Ministry of Transport sent to gather information about Pi's ordeal and the sinking of the *Tsimtsum*, Chiba is the junior colleague of Tomohiro Okamoto. He is the not as skeptical of Pi's tale as Okamoto. In the end, though, it is Okamoto who makes the final decision about which of the two stories appears in their official report.

The French Cook

The French cook becomes the human equivalent of the hyena when Pi remodels his version of the tale to suit the Japanese investigators, who do not believe Pi's initial tale. A violent and uncouth cannibal of a man, the cook kills the beautiful young sailor and then Pi's mother before he is killed by Pi in retaliation. As with most characters in the revised version of the story, there is much debate as to whether the cook is real or not.

The Hyena

One of the castaways aboard the lifeboat in Pi's first version of events, the hyena kills the zebra and then the orangutan before being killed in turn by the Royal Bengal tiger, Richard Parker. In the revised version of the story (the version without animals) the characteristics of the hyena are represented in the character of the French cook.

Satish Kumar

Sharing a name with Pi's high-school biology teacher, Satish Kumar is a Sufi, a Muslim mystic who works in a local bakery. An influential figure in Pi's development, Kumar is instrumental in leading Pi towards his lifelong interest in religion. When Satish Kumar visits the Patel family zoo, he sees the zoo animals as proof of the existence of a glorious god. He is a counterpoint to the almost identically named character of Mr. Satish Kumar, who is an atheist.

Mr. Satish Kumar

Pi's high-school biology teacher, Mr. Satish Kumar is an atheist and an active Communist, who was also afflicted with polio in his childhood. He inspires a love for empirical explanations of the world in Pi, and is a key figure in developing Pi's interest in zoology. When Mr. Kumar visits the Patel family zoo, he sees the way in which the animals have been arranged as proof of a scientific and rational logic. His character is a counterpoint to the other Satish Kumar, a devout Muslim.

Father Martin

Father Martin is the central figure in Pi's Christian education during the first part of the novel. His role is to offer comfort and guidance to Pi. His message is clear and well received by Pi; Martin states that the story of the Christian God is love and acceptance.

Tomohiro Okamoto

Tomohiro Okamoto is the lead investigator from the Maritime Department of the Japanese Ministry of Transport. He is in charge of the enquiry into the sinking of the *Tsimtsum*. Working with his assistant, Atsuro Chiba, he is the more suspicious of the two, as he is highly skeptical of the truthfulness of Pi's original story. He is also the final arbiter as to which version of events is included in his final report, the one with animals or the one without. The decision, Okamoto recalls when talking with the author, was both memorable and difficult. In the end, Okamoto chooses the story with animals, which, as indicated in the Author's Note, is the story that reinforces belief in the existence of God. To base his report on the story without animals would mean, also, that Okamoto readily accepts that the thin veneer of humanity crumbles into animalistic behavior almost immediately when placed outside of society (leading in this case to murder and cannibalism). Okamoto, like the author, prefers the story with animals to the dehumanizing and spiritually void alternative.

Orange Juice

Another of the castaways aboard the lifeboat in Pi's first version of events, Orange Juice is the prized Borneo orangutan whom Pi pulls into the lifeboat as she floats by on a raft of netted bananas. She is the second victim of the hyena, who turns on her after killing the zebra. Pi is particularly attached to Orange Juice, seeing her as a symbol of maternal affection and matriarchal protection (she attempts to protect the injured zebra, reminding him of his own mother who often acted as his protector). At the same time, Pi is taken aback when she lashes out violently at the hyena in the moments leading up to her death. In Pi's second version of events, Orange Juice is transformed to fill the role of Pi's mother.

Richard Parker

Richard Parker is the Royal Bengal tiger who shares the lifeboat with Pi following the sinking of the *Tsimtsum*. Originally named Thirsty, his name was changed through a clerical error that accidentally listed his captor's name as his own. A symbol of the ferocity of the natural world and of Pi's own unconscious, Parker is both a threat and a companion to Pi during their 227-day journey across the Pacific Ocean. Having already killed the hyena, Parker is an intelligent and brutal force that Pi must learn to control if the two are to coexist in the lifeboat. Whereas Pi is a man of faith and intellect, Parker sees the world as an animal does, guided by instinct and concerned mainly with hunger and thirst. It is he, for instance, who first recognizes the dangers of the algae island, returning to the boat every night to sleep safely away from the carnivorous algae. When the two companions finally arrive safely on a beach in Mexico, Parker disappears into the coastline jungle, leaving a void in Pi's emotional world. In Pi's second version of events, Richard Parker is transformed to represent Pi himself.

Gita Patel

Gita Patel is Pi's protective and loving mother. Raised a Hindu, but educated as a Baptist, she is, in many ways, a woman without formal religion, serving as a kind of counterpoint to Pi's seemingly perpetual quest for one. Through Gita, Pi learns to love reading. In the first version of Pi's story, she dies in the sinking of the *Tsimtsum*. In the second version, she is killed on the lifeboat by the French cook.

Meena Patel

Meena Patel is Pi's wife, whom the author meets very briefly while speaking with Pi in Toronto.

Nikhil Patel

Nikhil Patel, also known as Nick, is Pi's son. Defined primarily by his love of baseball, he is introduced to the author in a very brief meeting.

Pi Patel

Pi, born Piscine Molitor Patel, is the protagonist and first-person narrator of much of the novel. His name is derived from the French word for swimming pool (*piscine*) which rhymes uncomfortably with "pissing," prompting him to shorten it to the mathematical constant Pi.

In the chapters that constitute the first and third parts of the novel, Pi recounts both his upbringing at the Pondicherry zoo, his introduction to the religions of the world, and his later life in Toronto. Part Three also reveals his very open interpretation of reality and truth, as he willingly modifies his tale to appease the Japanese inspectors. But, as Pi reveals to them, the decision between the two stories is a relatively straightforward one: to believe in the story with animals is to believe in a world in which God can exist; but to believe in the story without animals is to be forced to acknowledge that human existence is nasty, brutish, and devoid of morality or spirituality.

In the substantive second part of the novel, Pi recounts his fabulous and often grisly story of survival. Sharing a lifeboat with a Royal Bengal tiger for 227 days, he finds that he is tested physically, intellectually, emotionally, and spiritually. Pi learns to fend off the natural impulses of fear and anger, as well as to allow those impulses to guide him (as in his hunting for food). He also learns that, in order to retain his sanity, he must achieve a deep personal honesty that allows him to acknowledge the animal within himself while still remaining human.

Piscine Molitor Patel

See Pi Patel

Ravi Patel

Ravi Patel is Pi's older brother. Where Pi is spiritual and intellectual, Ravi is athletic and social. He functions in the novel as a kind of foil to his younger brother. Through his relentless teasing, Ravi also tests Pi's developing religious beliefs.

Santosh Patel

Santosh Patel is Pi's father, who once owned a hotel in Madras before taking over the management of the Pondicherry zoo. Intrigued by animal culture and behavior, he passes his keen interest down to Pi. Due to the political climate in India during the years of the Emergency, Santosh decides to move his family to Canada. He dies when the cargo ship they are traveling on sinks into the Pacific.

Usha Patel

Usha Patel is Pi's shy but adoring daughter. The author meets her briefly.

The Sailor

In Pi's second version of events on the lifeboat, the sailor is the human equivalent of the zebra. The sailor is the French cook's first victim.

The Zebra

The zebra is one of the first animals on the lifeboat, and he is also the first animal that is killed by the hyena. In the revised version of Pi's tale, the zebra is represented by the sailor.

The Possibility of the Existence of God

When the author first meets Francis Adirubasamy in the opening chapter of *Life of Pi*, the elderly Indian man promises the somewhat skeptical writer that he has "a story that will make you believe in God." When the author later meets the central character in this story, an older Pi Patel now living in Toronto, he comes to understand that this assertion is very much at the crux of Pi's story.

Life of Pi offers readers two versions of the same story. One of these stories, which constitutes the bulk of the novel, includes a collection of wild animals and a floating carnivorous island. In this version, Pi is a man whose belief in God is put to the most profound tests as he is forced each day to try to remain civilized in a world bereft of human contact and in which basic survival is a challenge. In the end, it is his belief that sustains Pi, guiding him to forge an unlikely relationship with a Bengal tiger, to discover a discipline and strength within himself that allows him to survive each day at sea, and to recognize the dangers of an apparently idyllic island despite his deep desire to see it as a refuge.

The other story, considerably shorter than the version with animals, recounts a tale of murder and cannibalism. This story indicates that human goodness is a flimsy and easily removable construct.

Indeed, as both the author and the Japanese investigators conclude after hearing both of Pi's stories, the version with animals is the "better story," and it is also the most meaningful of the two. The "better story" is the story that represents a world where God might exist, but the other story represents a world that is spiritually void.

The Power of Storytelling

Constructed as a series of stories within a story, *Life of Pi* is a blend of various storytelling forms, from first-person accounts (both by Pi and by the author) that move forward and backward in time, to the emotionally intense internal monologues and the ostensibly factual interview transcripts. Each form of storytelling is revealed within the novel to contain its own version of truth and accuracy, with none of the many stories able to explain exactly all that had happened aboard the lifeboat. With each new story, few answers are provided while more and more questions are raised.

Topics for Further Study

- Given that the Patel family leaves Pondicherry during the period of Indian history known as the Emergency, research the history of this period in India. Write an essay in which you comment on the relevance of this period to the journey that Pi is later forced to take following the sinking of the *Tsimtsum*. In your essay, consider the question: Do you think that *Life of Pi* can be read, in part, as a political commentary on such issues as political territoriality or the animal nature of human politics? Why? Why not?

- *Life of Pi* is a novel that is full of colors: the yellow of bananas; the orange of the orangutan and the Royal Bengal tiger; the blue of the sea and sky. Write an essay in which you discuss the meanings of each of the various colors mentioned in the book, and the importance of what or whom they are attached to.

- In chapter 58, Pi spends some time reading a survival manual that he discovers on the lifeboat. Written by a British Royal Navy commander, it is an eclectic collection of obvious and not-so-obvious hints for survival. Write a similar manual for surviving life as a student. Include at least twelve items, making some of the points practical and others more abstract. Feel free to include diagrams, calculations, or images if the mood strikes you.

- In chapter 5, Pi goes to great lengths to have his name translated from the embarrassing Piscine to the more liberating Pi, which is both a Greek letter and almost mythical mathematical constant. Research the visual art and music that has accumulated around this number, and create a timeline of paintings, cartoons, and musical scores (as examples) that have been inspired by this number. What information can you find about the number that indicates its spiritual significance? Present your findings to the class.

- The novel is a sly argument promoting spiritual belief, specifically belief in God. What other philosophers have also attempted to argue that God exists? Compile a report on your findings and include a brief description of each philosopher's argument.

Rather than collapsing the story into a debate about a solid and knowable set of facts or certainties regarding Pi's adventures (what might be called reality), *Life of Pi* opens outwards to explore other ways of seeing and knowing the world. When Pi meets his Japanese investigators, for instance, he offers them two very different but intimately related versions of the same tale, one with animals and the other without. Both versions are true in their own way. In the end, the decision as to what version to believe is left to Okamoto and Chida, and, more importantly, to the reader of the novel itself.

Echoing such earlier stories as told in Samuel Taylor Coleridge's poem "The Rime of the Ancient Mariner" (1798), *Life of Pi* is also a novel that explores the human need to tell and believe in stories as a strategy for survival. As Pi explains often during the opening section of the novel, the various stories that shape world religions are necessary for human survival. Each of Pi's three religions has its own distinct set of stories (often shaped as parables) and narrative strategies. What Pi comes to understand about this plethora of stories is very profound: all of the stories, in the end, address a deeply rooted need to love and be loved, and in order to survive in the world every individual needs to put his faith in one or another story of this (divine) love. To remain an agnostic is to live without faith in the power of stories to shape one's very existence in meaningful ways.

The Conditions of Human Nature

The Pondicherry zoo serves as an important reminder of the distinctions separating human beings from wild animals. Yet the zoo also makes Pi aware of some similarities between the two. Just as animals find some solace in the rituals of zoo life, Pi believes that humans find solace in the rituals of daily life. The order and structure of the zoo comes to represent the human ability to bring order and harmony to a primitive world that is always on the cusp of reverting back to a natural, wild state. In its wild state, life is a constant struggle for survival, a perpetual race for food and safety in which death is a constant possibility.

As Pi's journey aboard the lifeboat begins, so, too, does his reeducation in the conditions of wildness and human nature. After witnessing the savagery of the hyena, Pi comes to realize that the world in which he now lives has been stripped of the false comforts and artificial harmonies of society. This new world is one in which his faith will be profoundly tested. As he learns to live peacefully with, rather than in fear of, Richard Parker, for instance, Pi also begins to recognize, much to his disappointment, that his own behaviors are becoming more animal-like. Pi learns to kill fish and turtles without any sort of guilt, for instance. He not only drinks their blood and eats their brains in order to survive, but he does so with an almost bestial gusto. At first, Pi is appalled when he catches himself wolfing down a new catch of food, but he gradually comes to recognize how easy it is for him to slip away from the religion and vegetarianism that had defined his early life, and how easy it is to live a life that is discomfortingly similar to that of the zoo animals he had once tended.

Gradually, the distance separating Pi from Richard Parker is almost erased in the novel. Readers are left with the possibility that Parker and Pi are distinct but connected elements of the same character, with the tiger emerging as a symbol of Pi's primal nature and his instinctive drive for survival at all costs. If readers accept that the second version of Pi's story is true, then the invention of Richard Parker can be understood as a psychological mechanism that allows Pi to disassociate himself from the murder that he has committed. Read in either of these ways, the novel underscores what such writers as Joseph Conrad (*Heart of Darkness*, 1902) and William Golding (*Lord of the Flies*, 1954) had explored previously:

that humans are not so different from animals as is traditionally believed. Deprived of the zoo-like structures (society) that sustain them in their daily lives, humans return quite naturally to lives guided by basic instincts and animalistic impulses.

Magical Realism

The term was first used by the German art critic Franz Roh to describe paintings that present recognizable objects in an altered form or setting. More specifically, these works of art represented a kind of heightened reality in which elements of the marvelous or the unnatural appear alongside familiar elements of the everyday world.

In literature, including in *Life of Pi*, magical realism often blurs the familiar line between the internal/emotional world of the characters and the external/physical world through which these characters move. Serving as a literary counterpoint to traditional beliefs in a unified and knowable reality shared by all people and all cultures, magical realism acknowledges that everyday reality is a relative concept, and that what is seen as real or normal by one individual might at the same moment be seen as miraculous or magical by another. Promoting an openness to other ways of seeing the world and underscoring the need for tolerance of divergent opinions, magical realism has become increasingly important in a world fractured by territorial and cultural tensions.

The emergence of Richard Parker as an almost-human personality in the novel, for instance, and the floating, carnivorous island (which at first seems to be a paradise), mark *Life of Pi* as a novel written in the tradition of magical realism. Accordingly, *Life of Pi* can be read alongside works by such international writers as Isabel Allende (*The House of Spirits*, 1982) Italo Calvino (*Invisible Cities*, 1972) and Salman Rushdie (*Midnight's Children*, 1981) to name but a few.

Bildungsroman

The novel traces the intellectual, spiritual, and physical Maturation of Pi Patel, and thus falls very neatly into the tradition of the Bildungsroman, a novel tracing the formation or education of its (typically male) protagonist. Known alternatively as the coming-of-age novel, the Bildungsroman in its more organized form usually includes a number of elements, most of which appear in whole or in part in Martel's novel. The protagonist grows during the course of the novel from a boy into a man; Pi leaves India as a sixteen-year-old and recounts his story to the author many years later, as an older man living in Toronto with his family. The protagonist must also have an obvious motivation for undertaking his transformative journey, which for Pi can be seen as both the political implications of the Emergency and the more immediate motivation for survival following the sinking of the *Tsimtsum*.

In a Bildungsroman, once the journey is underway the protagonist must face a long and arduous trial (227 days in a lifeboat) that is punctuated with a conflict between his needs and those of others within his community (Pi versus Richard Parker). As the journey unfolds, the protagonist of the Bildungsroman traditionally grows away from a spirit of conformity towards a more individualized sense of the world and his place in it. Finally, as is apparent throughout *Life of Pi*, there is a thematic emphasis on the spiritual or the emotional and the practical problems associated with living outside of social norms. Mark Twain's *Huckleberry Finn* (1885) is a classic example of a Bildungsroman.

The Emergency Years in Indian History

When Santosh Patel decides to leave Pondicherry for a better life in Canada, he openly cites the political unrest that was sweeping India in the mid-1970s as his motivation to emigrate. The period known formally as the Emergency was a twenty-one-month period beginning on June 25, 1975, and ending around March 21, 1977. During this period, Indian President Fakhruddin Ali Ahmed, responding to the advice of Prime Minister Indira Gandhi, declared a state of emergency throughout India. Rooted in long-standing political disagreements and widespread disillusionment with policies of the day, the declaration effectively granted the Government the power to rule by decree and without pressure to recognize civil liberties or the due process of democratic elections.

Also during this time, the Government deployed its police forces to suppress protests and strikes, banned many parties that offered political opposition, and engaged in a sustained attempt to rewrite Indian laws with the sanction of Parliament.

The legacy of this period remains controversial. Although economic recovery was strengthened and the political climate of the country was stabilized through many of the decisions put into place, the Emergency years are also seen as a black mark against India's commitment to the principles of democratic rule.

The Rise of Post-Colonialism

Post-Colonialism refers to a collection of theories and critical approaches that look to explore the culture of countries that were once ruled by foreign governments (India is a former British colony). Although more a collection of ideas than a single, unified theory, post-colonialism does feature a number of common subjects that arise in *Life of Pi*: the heritage of European influences in local art, philosophy, and religion; racism; political territoriality; and the struggle for cultural identity. The beginnings of post-colonial thinking is mostly considered to have come from two writers: Frantz Fanon (*Black Skin, White Masks*, 1952) and Edward Said (*Orientalism*, 1978). Both men had a powerful influence on the intellectual climate of the 1970s.

One of the key strategies of post-colonial thinkers is to consider how the colonizer's culture has become hybridized in the culture of the colonized. The merging of old with new, colonizing with pre-colonial, is seen as creating something particularly unique to the post-colonial culture, and serves as a foundation for future growth. Pi Patel's bringing together of elements of Christianity, Hinduism, and Islam is an excellent example of what post-colonial thinkers would call a hybridized identity. Taking bits and pieces from old and new aspects of his culture, Pi positions himself as both a man of the past and a beacon of the emergence of that past into a new, hopefully progressive future. Indeed, Pi is a post-colonial figure. The fact that he resists traditional pressures to choose one path serves only to underscore both the limitations (territoriality) of the old ways and the necessity for an inclusive view of the world.

Significantly, *Life of Pi* resists the tendency of most post-colonial writing to settle too easily on a new, hybridized identity as the solution to all problems. What Pi discovers on his journey across the Pacific Ocean is that even his hybridized faith cannot answer all of the questions that confront him.

Somewhat surprisingly, given its meteoric rise as a novel of international standing, *Life of Pi* was greeted with what a contributor to the *Missouri Review* characterizes as "wildly disparate reactions." Writing in the *New York Review of Books*, for instance, Pankaj Mishra gives the novel only the mildest of praise. Mishra celebrates Martel's skill in "stretch[ing] our credulity through some hypnotic storytelling." The critic, however, is troubled by Martel's depictions of religious life generally and his "unpersuasive treatment of God" more specifically. The description of religious practices in India, for instance, "carry the whiff of an encyclopedia entry, or a tourist's scrupulously kept journal," while later in the novel "Martel is unable to reveal adequately ... the precise nature, or vacillations, of Pi's faith." In the end, Mishra concludes, Martel's "instincts as a storyteller prove to be keener than his ability to proselytize" in support of a new way of making God relevant in an increasingly secular world. As Linda M. Morra concludes in *Canadian Literature*, *Life of Pi* is, for many readers, "inconsistently compelling and occasionally contrived."

Reviewing the novel for the *Christian Century*, Gordon Houser is far less hesitant in his praise of Martel's exploration of questions of a spiritual nature. Noting that the writing is "deceptively simple," Houser celebrates the "aplomb" with which

"Martel lets the winsome narrative voice and the intriguing plot carry [readers], all the while winking as he tosses out thoughts on the kinds of metaphysical questions humans have pondered for centuries." Indeed, they are questions, notes Linda Shirato in *Library Journal* that tend to elicit "strong emotions" from most readers. This point is also made by Charlotte Innes, writing in the *Nation*. Martel "baits his readers with serious themes and trawls them through a sea of questions and confusion," she begins, "but he makes one laugh so much, and at times feel so awed and chilled, that even thrashing around in bewilderment or disagreement one can't help but be captured by his prose." Aligning the novel with such classic castaway tales as Defoe's *Robinson Crusoe* and Swift's *Gulliver's Travels*, Innes is ebullient in her praise: "above all," she writes, this is "a book about life's absurdities that makes one laugh out loud on almost every page, with its quirky juxtapositions, comparisons, metaphors, Borgesian puzzles, postmodern games and a sense of fun that reflects the hero's sensual enjoyment of the world."

Comparisons alleging plagiarism have been drawn between *Life of Pi* and Brazilian author Moacyr Scliar's *Max and the Cats* (1981), an earlier book that shows remarkable similarities with Martel's novel. The various accounts about this are somewhat convoluted, but supposedly Martel mentioned that he had been intrigued by the premise of Scliar's novel after reading an unfavorable review of it by American novelist John Updike in the *New York Times Book Review*. Martel soon came under fire when it was shown that no such review existed and Updike publicly stated that he had no knowledge whatsoever of the Brazilian novel. Martel claims never to have read Scliar's book, despite the fact that the Author's Note in *Life of Pi* includes thanks to Mr. Moacyr Scliar "for the spark of life." The story has it that Scliar considered a lawsuit but changed his mind after personally speaking with Martel.

Sources

Houser, Gordon, Review of *Life of Pi*, in the *Christian Century*, February 8, 2003, pp. 34-35.

Innes, Charlotte, "Robinson Crusoe, Move Over," in the *Nation*, August 19-26, 2002, pp. 25-29.

Iyer, Pico, "The Last Refuge," in *Harper's* magazine, Vol. 304, No. 1825, 2002, pp. 77-80.

Martel, Yann, *Life of Pi*, Vintage Canada, 2002.

Mishra, Pankaj, "The Man or the Tiger?" in the *New York Review of Books*, Vol. 50, No. 5, March 27, 2003, pp. 43-54.

Morra, Linda M., Review of *Life of Pi*, in *Canadian Literature*, Vol. 177, Summer 2003, p. 163.

Review of *Life of Pi*, in the *Missouri Review*, Vol. 27, No. 1, 2004, pp. 179-80.

Shirato, Linda, Review of *Life of Pi*, in *Library Journal*, May 15, 2003, p. 164.

Further Reading

Ashcroft, Bill, Gareth Griffiths, and Helen Tiffin, *The Empire Writes Back: Theory and Practice in Post-Colonial Literatures*, Routledge, 2002.

> This was the first major theoretical account of a wide range of post-colonial texts and their relation to the larger issues of post-colonial culture, and remains one of the most significant works published in this field.

Moretti, Franco, *The Way of the World: The Bildungsroman in European Culture*, Verso Books, 2000.

> This seminal study positions the Bildungsroman as the great cultural mediator of nineteenth-century Europe, arguing that the form explores the many strange compromises between revolution and restoration; economic transition and aesthetic pleasure; and individual autonomy and social normality.

New, William H., ed., *Encyclopedia of Literature in Canada*, University of Toronto Press, 2002.

> This book is an invaluable reference companion to the literatures of Canada, and it discusses Canadian

authors and their work, related literary and social issues, and the major historical and cultural events that have shaped Canadian literature.

Said, Edward W., *Orientalism*, Vintage, 1979.

The Eastern world was first known to the West only through literature and texts that viewed it, for the most part, through a predominantly Western perspective. The crux of this study is a critique of how the academic world has regarded the East and how they have only helped to legitimize and feed this skewed perspective.

Printed in February 2022
by Rotomail Italia S.p.A., Vignate (MI) - Italy